PUBLIC SPEAKING
Magic

SUCCESS AND CONFIDENCE
IN THE FIRST 20 SECONDS

MARK DAVIS & TOM "BIG AL" SCHREITER

For information, contact:

Fortune Network Publishing
PO Box 890084
Houston, TX 77289 USA

Telephone: +1 (281) 280-9800

ISBN: 1-892366-47-9

ISBN-13: 978-1-892366-47-4

Thank you for reading this book.

Below are two resources as our gift to you.

#1. Here is a free audio by Coach Mark Davis to help you with public speaking. Just go to this site to download it now:

http://www.markdavis.com.au/books/

#2. If you are involved in network marketing, download our free chart of the "25 Skills for Network Marketers." Plus, you can get fresh tips on building your business free in the "Big Al" Reports.

http://www.BigAlReport.com/25skills.PDF

#3. Finally, if you would like a public speaking workshop in your city, or for your group, contact Coach Mark Davis directly at:

Mark@MasterTheArtOfPublicSpeaking.com

TABLE OF CONTENTS

PREFACE

Never given a speech before? Nervous?

Totally understandable. This book can help put our minds at ease. We will learn how to eliminate two of the biggest fears when it comes to public speaking.

Do you give speeches now?

This book won't cover the history of public speaking, or go on endlessly about how to fine-tune body postures. We will show you three ways to open our speeches that will make us look great.

All three shortcuts will immediately help us remove our fear of public speaking and get our message across easily. And, as an added benefit, our audience will love us.

This is not a book that covers the entire subject of public speaking. This book only focuses on creating a great opening. Then, the rest of our speech is easy. Our audience loves us.

– Mark Davis and Tom "Big Al" Schreiter

Why public speaking is scary.

The two biggest fears of public speaking are:

#1. Forgetting what to say next. We don't want to look like an idiot staring into space.

#2. Our audience won't like us and will tell other people how bad we are.

Nobody likes looking stupid and nobody likes rejection. If we can eliminate these two big fears, we can deliver a great speech with no stress.

Brand-new to public speaking? No problem.

Intimidated by an audience? No problem.

Experienced in public speaking? Great. Then you will enjoy these three shortcuts to help you deliver your message even better.

The late George Jessel said it best, "The human brain starts working the moment you are born and never stops until you stand up to speak in public."

Speeches come in many formats and situations. Here are just a few situations where we might want to be a compelling speaker:

1. A sales presentation.

7

2. A business meeting or conference.

3. A formal dinner.

4. Best man at a wedding.

5. As the emcee for an awards banquet.

6. A fundraising presentation.

7. A public assembly.

We all want to be better. We all want better results. So, let's get ready for our audience to love us.

Our first 20 seconds overview.

The first 20 seconds are very scary. We all know the old saying, "First impressions are everything."

Here is why we should be scared. Like it or not, every speaker is cruelly judged in the first 20 seconds. Our audience automatically thinks:

* Who is this person?

* Why should I listen to this person?

* Does this person have credibility?

* Why should I pay attention?

* Maybe I should be texting on my phone.

* Does this person really know what he is talking about?

* Am I wasting my time?

* Maybe I should go to the bathroom.

* I wonder if this person will ever get to the point.

* Will this person say something of value for me?

* Is this person self-centered and egotistical?

* Will I be entertained?

* Do I like the way this person dresses?

* Do I like this person?

* Why do I have to sit through another boring speech?

Yes, the audience can be cruel. There is a good reason we feel nervous when we first start a public speech.

However...

* What if we knew exactly how to start our speech?

* What if it was impossible to forget what we were going to say?

* What if we knew exactly how to get our audience to forget all the negative thoughts above, and totally focus on our message?

Now, we are confident. We have less stress. And we can deliver our message to an audience wanting to hear what we have to say.

This is the most important part of our speech.

Get the first 20 seconds right, and the rest is easy.

Get the first 20 seconds wrong, and we will sweat like an Eskimo eating a spicy Thai curry.

Want some examples of starting wrong?

Bad opening. "Hi, uh, today I will tell you..."

What is the audience thinking? Oh no. Another person lecturing to us. Boring and condescending.

Not-so-good opening. "Hello, how is everyone feeling today?"

The audience is thinking, "Oh no, I have to respond to this speaker with fake happiness and enthusiasm. Where's my phone so I can avoid eye contact?"

Worse opening. "Hi. I have a bit of a cough today, so please bear with me. A bit nervous here as I normally don't speak to groups. I can't read my notes as my dog ate them on my way to the venue..."

Oh, my. The audience already has an attitude, and the future isn't looking good either.

Near-death opening. "You might be wondering why you should listen to me today. So let me spend the next 20 minutes telling you about my accomplishments and why I am so great."

Our audience thinks, "Another egotistical, selfish, all-about-me-and-my-accomplishments speech, just to make me feel inferior."

Want to do better? This is the solution.

The three shortcuts that will make us look great.

Here are the three shortcuts to incredible openings that we will master in this book.

1. Ask a question.

2. Tell a story.

3. Do an exercise.

Simple. Now, let's learn exactly what to say to use make these shortcuts work for us.

Shortcut #1: Ask a question.

The human mind can only entertain one thought at a time.

We can control which thought our audience has in their minds.

Remember those negative thoughts the audience had in the previous chapter? These are automatic thoughts. Our audience will be questioning our value and the value of our speech automatically... unless we give them a different thought!

How do we give the audience a different thought?

By asking them a question.

Any question.

The audience has to forget their automatic thoughts about judging us. We want our audience to focus on the question we ask. Their minds will be searching for the answer to our question. And those automatic negative thoughts they had? Completely forgotten.

Look how easy this is. For example, ask:

"Do you put on your left shoe
before your right shoe?"

Now, what is the audience thinking? Their minds have rolled back to visualize which shoe they put on first in the morning. They think, "I wonder what that says about me?"

That was easy, wasn't it?

Here is another example.

"Have you ever felt embarrassed when you
try to talk to a stranger?"

Again, what is the audience thinking? Their minds return to that place and time where they were embarrassed when approaching a stranger. Again, they are engaged. They wonder if we will be solving that problem for them. We have the audience thinking the thoughts we want them to think, not their automatic thoughts about judging us as the speaker.

Questions: The fast track to
getting our audience to like us.

Questions are an easy way to grab our audience's favorable attention. By asking a question first, the audience feels they will get valuable information to solve that question. They feel engaged. It is almost as if we are having a **conversation** with them.

When we ask a question, everyone listens. They don't have to agree, or even answer out loud. But, they will listen. This is great for us as the speaker. Now the

14

audience focuses on the present question, not on us or themselves.

Using a follow-up question engages our audience even further. It reinforces our opening question. More on that later.

Finally in this section, we will list seven easy starter questions. These examples will give us openings for hundreds of talks, guaranteed.

Questions: We have to know the answer!

One quick word of caution. Make sure we know the answer to our own question. That is just common sense. Our opening question engages our audience's minds and takes away their judgment of us. So let's also make sure our opening question is about our message.

Questions: No response needed.

Don't worry if the audience knows the answer to our question, or if they don't respond.

The purpose of our opening question is to simply get the audience's minds focused on something other than judging us.

If the audience shouts out an answer, fine. If the audience is silent and ponders our question, fine. We simply continue with our speech, as our opening question has introduced our message.

Here are 30 examples of opening questions to give us more ideas.

Let's start with easy examples and gradually build up our "question muscles." We will then use our creativity and modify some of these questions for our next speech.

Question #28 outlines a simple formula to create the first full 20 seconds of our speech. Just think of this as one template to start our speech, not as the only template.

1. "Do you feel afraid when calling cold prospects?"

Every salesman in the room feels that we understand them. Even though this is a simple "yes or no" question, our audience is thinking about our question. If we have non-salesmen in our audience, they feel petrified about sales calls. We have their instant attention.

2. "Would you like to know what your stomach is really doing while you are sleeping?"

Curiosity will grab our audience's attention. Most audiences won't remember their high school science class. This sounds like a fun bit of information to share with their friends over coffee break. Want to be perceived as the expert? A couple of visual slides can make us look awesome.

3. "Did you ever talk to someone and feel like the other person wasn't listening?"

This is fun to do when the audience isn't paying attention to us. The audience that is listening, will laugh. Because these people are laughing, the other part of the audience that wasn't listening will instantly turn their attention to us. Almost everyone has felt their message was ignored in the past. You are bonding with the audience through a common experience.

4. "Have you ever caught yourself 'frozen in time' with everything in slow motion?"

Now would be a good time to pause for a few seconds, and let our audience feel "frozen in time." Everyone can think of a time when they were so mesmerized by something they saw, that they stared, and felt "frozen in time."

5. "When was the last time you woke up on a Sunday morning without a hangover?"

Good opening for a group of party animals, but maybe not the best opening question for a religious organization. There is no one-size-fits-all opening sentence. If we see our audience struggle at a corporate retreat, workshop or conference because of Saturday night's banquet, this would be an appropriate opening. There will be heads nodding and smiles from our audience who feel that we understand them.

6. "When was the last time you woke up without feeling stiff and sore?"

Older people will naturally feel that we understand them. This is also great for gym enthusiasts that push their bodies to the limit. What happens inside our audience's minds when we ask this question? They think, "Wow. You understand me. I like you."

7. "Who is the first person you think of when you hear the word 'success?'"

The audience's minds wander into their memories to pick a person. You don't even need to suggest a person. Everyone has an idol, a mentor, a guide or an "ideal" person they respect. It will bring up feelings of aspiration, adoration and sometimes even competition. Great for leading into a workshop or training on becoming successful.

8. "What is the first thing you will buy when you have all your debts paid off?"

Now, our listeners feel excited. They want to hear how they will get that money. They have a mental list already. We can continue to engage our audience and ask for volunteers to share what they would buy. Everyone wants to know what others choose. We have their undivided attention. Because it is all about them!

9. "Where is the first place you would take a vacation if you had an extra $10,000?"

We like to dream. As we go into our dream, our negative thoughts about the speaker fade away. All the focus on traffic, parking, babysitters, the temperature of the room - all gone in a moment. People love to jump into another place and time with their thoughts. We made that happen. Great to use when we are helping the audience make more money or save money.

10. "Who would you rate as your #1 teacher in high school?"

The audience quickly calculates the ranking of the teachers they liked. The audience thinks, "Why did I like this teacher? What will this have to do with the talk? Maybe I will learn why some people are influential, popular, charismatic, or confident. Maybe I will learn how to be respected by others."

Starting to get the idea?

Yes, questions totally occupy that "one thought at a time" space inside our audience's heads. Now we are in control of what the audience is thinking. They engage. They listen to us. We replace all those negative automatic judgments that audiences have about speakers.

Let's continue now with a huge variety of questions. Certainly one of these questions can be modified to be the opening of our next speech.

11. "Are you a 'morning person' or a 'night person?'"

Our audience quickly takes sides to our question, and then starts to prepare in their minds why they are right. Our audience is totally engaged, ready for debate. As the speaker, we could talk about the advantages or disadvantages of both. Feel comfortable with humor? We could exaggerate the characteristics and experiences of both the morning person and the night person.

12. "Where do you go when you want to feel motivated?"

Probably not a good opening question when speaking to a corporate workforce. Their answer is probably anywhere but the workplace! This is a great opening for overwhelmed young mothers, stressed entrepreneurs, or unmotivated students.

13. "How many cups of coffee do you need in the morning to feel human?"

Nice opening if we show up with a giant cup of coffee. A great lead-in question if we are speaking about health or even stress. People love coffee. We are talking about something they love. They have to like us.

14. "How old is your phone?"

We can use this question in three ways.

First, we can lead in to the rapid growth of technology and our inability to keep up.

Second, what does our phone model say about us as a person? Do we have the latest phone to impress people who don't care? Do we have the original mobile phone from 1990?

Third, are we afraid of change?

15. "What is the most money you ever earned in a single day?"

Our listeners will be thinking, "What? Why is the speaker asking this? Is there a chance I could earn more? Am I missing something? Yes, tell me more." We have their attention. And it is **favorable** attention.

This opening question should help us relax. Our listeners lean forward in their chairs, waiting for the explanation that will come next. At this point, we could start a story leading up to our first big earning day.

16. "Orange juice, yogurt, breakfast cereal, and whole wheat pancakes. Which one of these four foods will kill you fastest? The answer might surprise you."

In this example, we put a bit more information into our opening. Please note, it is the question that will freeze their minds. They are thinking, "Okay, don't pick the obvious choice. But yes, the answer is going to surprise me. I like surprises." We take our audience hand-in-hand and lead them through our presentation. We bond with them. They love us because they learn something that can save their lives.

17. "Do you know what our lovely bride and groom were doing exactly five years ago today?"

Most of the time, the best man has to make a short speech before toasting the bride and groom at the wedding reception. The best man is a friend, not a professional speaker. With no idea how to start, the best man stresses for days before the wedding on what to say first. The above question is a great opener for the toast. The wedding party is curious for the answer. The focus is off of the sweating best man who can barely hold his drink steady, and the focus is on what happened exactly five years ago.

18. "If you got fired today, how long could you live without a regular paycheck? One month? Three months? One year?"

The audience quickly does some calculations in their head. Then they wonder, "What is the solution? How can we avoid this? How can we have more security?" We are now walking down the same path as the audience, looking for answers to those questions.

19. "What is your dream job?"

A bad opening to a corporate audience being forced to listen to our speech. But this is a great opening to unemployed people looking for a better future. The promise of our question is that we will tell the audience how to get that dream job. That is what this audience wants, and we are going to deliver it. From the front of the room, we can feel the bonding with the audience. We are in total rapport. Nothing feels better than that.

20. "What is your top habit for personal time management?"

Most people have only one habit for time management: Procrastination. They hate that. However, they don't have any other habits to replace procrastination. They know they need better habits and are anxiously looking forward to the tips.

Are you starting to feel more comfortable?

As we can see from these opening questions, our audience quickly forgets about us. Instead, they concentrate on how the question affects their lives. People care about themselves, not us. Now we should feel relieved. They are thinking about their problems and solutions, and they want to hear our message.

At this point, with just a simple starting question, we will feel more relaxed. We will sense the audience connecting with us. Our message can now go directly to their minds, without them judging us.

Ready for some more questions to give us more opening ideas?

21. "Who is better-looking? The person on your right? The person on your left? Or you?"

This opening is fun. Everyone in our audience will look at the person on their right and on their left. Lots of smiles, lots of laughs. And the audience gets to participate. They can do something instead of just listening to us.

Humor is a great way to bond with our audience, and we didn't even take the risk of telling a joke. As an added bonus, it will take the audience ten seconds or more to do their looking and laughing. That gives us a bit of time to take a sip of water, a deep breath, and calm our nerves. We will feel much better when we get our audience participating and laughing at the start.

22. "Which car you would drive if price was no object?"

If we have PowerPoint slides, now would be a good time to have a slide with four different types of cars. If we are comfortable with humor, we could show a picture of a tiny car from 50 years ago. Some people like the classics, while others would love a brand-new Ferrari or luxury car. The audience is thinking, "So what does my choice of cars tell me about myself? And 'me' is my favorite subject!"

23. "How many chances do you get to make a first impression?"

Okay, it is a rhetorical question, but the audience will still answer it in their minds. Now they are wondering what they can do to make better first impressions. They want us to deliver the solutions. I use this question often in my presentations and public speaking.

24. "What is the biggest mistake you have made in your life... so far?"

If we are comfortable with humor, then add, "And you are only allowed one." Then, smile and pause.

Don't ask for the audience to volunteer answers. We don't want the audience to feel depressed. But our audience is thinking about themselves, their favorite topic. They are reviewing past disasters in relationships, business, sports and more. We have the audience involved.

Now, we give the audience a few seconds to think about the question. Then, we can easily follow up with, "And what lesson did you learn from that failure?" Again, the audience is thinking about what they learned. An involved audience is a happy audience. We are having a **conversation** with them instead of preaching and talking at them.

25. "If today was the last day of your life, what would you do right now?"

Oh, my. The thoughts start streaming into our audience's minds. "Would I quickly write my will? Would I run out of here and get drunk? Would I rob a bank? Would I apologize to someone I hurt?" Instant-reaction questions are great for group interaction, as the responses can be inspiring or sometimes hilarious.

26. "What is your best excuse for not exercising?"

Smiles from those who are out-of-shape in the audience. We can follow up with some humorous excuses and now they know the talk will be fun. Think of some humorous examples why people don't exercise. If we can't, just search that term on the Internet to get some witty excuses for our talk.

Think about the connection we will have with this question. The audience has excuses not to exercise, and we acknowledge that people have excuses. One of the best ways to create rapport is by agreeing with the audience's current beliefs.

So remember, if we want our audience to feel that we are just like them, ask a question, or tell a fact that is congruent with their current beliefs.

27. "What do you do when you need an energy boost?"

We can continue this question with a bit of discovery by saying, "Some people grab an energy drink or pill, some people gulp down a double expresso. But did you know that a short burst of exercise works better?"

The audience loves learning new things they can share with their friends in conversation. An opening such as this tells our audience they will discover interesting facts. Try to incorporate a bit of discovery in openings to get our audience to lean forward, waiting for our next announcement or scientific discovery. When we quote independent scientific research, well, the audience knows that it must be true. No reason to doubt us.

Want to expand our opening question a bit more?

Let's look at a little formula to complete our first 20 seconds. Here is our first example.

28. "How do you relax and remove stress?"

Again, continue with some options by saying, "Do you meditate? Do you mindlessly watch television? Do you try to get away from it all with a long walk in nature? Or would you like to discover a new, scientifically-proven way to remove stress in less than 60 seconds?"

Wow. In this example, we have done three things.

A. We asked a question to get our audience thinking about how they handle their personal stress. Takes their minds off of us.

B. We bonded with the audience by talking about common ways people cope with stress. Certainly one of these ways will resonate with them, and they will feel that they think the way you think. You have established good rapport.

C. And then we promised an interesting discovery. The audience wants to know more right away.

This opening took about 20 seconds! This is a great formula for starting any speech:

A. Ask a question.

B. Bond with our audience by sharing a common feeling.

C. Promise an interesting discovery.

With a little bit of professional planning, you can accomplish a lot in 20 seconds. Compare the previous opening to random openings from a nervous and unsure speaker. With a great opening, we will feel confident.

Want another example?

29. "What makes you buy things?"

What is the audience thinking? They start to look inside their minds for triggers that cause them to buy some things, and not to buy other things.

Continue by saying, "Does advertising manipulate your mind? Do you want something because people you know have it already? Are you influenced by the recommendations of friends? Do pushy salesmen make you feel guilty? Well, psychologists now know the exact process that causes us to want to buy things. Prepare to be surprised."

We know everyone in our audience wants to know this exact process. They don't care about the speaker's background or how tall they are, or how many degrees they have.

They just want to know the answer.

We bond with our audience by asking questions that interest them. The promise of discovering the answers to our original questions creates suspense and attention.

As the audience leans forward, smile. People are reciprocal. When we smile, they will too. Everyone is happy.

One more example.

30. "What kind of music do you listen to?"

Continue with, "Music from your teenage years? Hip Hop? Rock 'n Roll? Heavy metal? Pop? Your music preference can predict how you react to stressful situations. So, which music do you like the most?"

This is getting personal, and the audience loves it. We are talking about them, and it doesn't get any more interesting than that. They want to know the answer to how they will naturally react to stress. This is also a great conversation starter with their friends and colleagues after our talk is over.

Our first 20 seconds, if professionally prepared, make the rest of our speech easy.

By carefully starting with an opening question, and then following up with a few scripted sentences, we put the odds in our favor. We now have the best chance of getting the audience to think about our topic instead of thinking about us. Plus, we have the best chance that they will love us as a speaker.

As speakers, we know the challenge. We can plan for that challenge by creating specific sentences that get our audiences to think about our message, instead of judging us.

But, what if you are extremely shy?

We might think, "I don't have the confidence to start my speech with a direct question to the audience."

No problem.

We can make our questions more conversational. Use this example as a template.

"While I was sitting in the back of the room before we started, I wondered, 'How many people here today are just like me? They want to exercise. They know exercise is important. But no matter how hard they try, the motivation just isn't there.'"

Or, say something like this:

"When I landed here in New York City yesterday, I thought to myself, 'How can somebody live here?' But then I remembered that eight million people already live here. And, they love it. So what makes New York City so addictive to these people?"

By making the opening question more conversational, we draw people into a miniature story about us. It works. Our audience will love it. But more about stories later.

For now, here are 21 examples of using an opening question in a more conversational manner.

21 more examples of opening questions.

1. "I just noticed this glass of water has little things floating in it. Do you want to guess what those things are?"

2. "During the break, I was talking to John here on the front row. Would you like to know the real reason John came to this conference?"

3. "They ran out of donuts during the break. Sad. But did you realize that this is the only hotel in the city that makes its own donuts?"

4. "Yes, I have known the groom since we sat together in first grade. But do you know what really surprised me when he said he got engaged?"

5. "I look at the number of smartphones in this room, and remember that 20 years ago only one in 1000 people even had email addresses. Isn't it fascinating how much change in technology has occurred in our lifetime?"

6. "You think you are the most fascinating person here today. But that is just because you haven't met Mandy, the event coordinator. Do you know what she did for five years before this job?"

7. "Take a look at where you are sitting today. Are you in the front? The back? Would you like to know what your choice of a seat today tells you about yourself?"

8. "Before Peter introduced me today, your program director cornered me backstage. He was mad, really mad. Would you like to know why?"

9. "Look at the pitcher of water at your table. That water has been recycled seven times. Before you drink your water, would you like to know where it came from originally?"

10. "I parked my car earlier, opened my door, and dented the car next to me. Would you like to know if that car was yours?"

11. "When I opened my bag of potato chips during the break, the most enticing aroma emerged. Do the chemists here in the room know which chemical creates that aroma?"

12. "Well, the World Cup is officially over. Depressing to some, opportunity for others. Did you know that the sales of anti-depressants soar immediately after the World Cup?"

13. "Like most of you, I was stuck in traffic coming here today. So I took my time, looked at the other drivers. Do you know what most of them were doing with their index finger?"

14. "Driving here today, I had to follow an overweight cyclist wearing Lycra, stretched to the limits. Do you think there should be rules about who can wear Lycra in public?"

15. "Your CEO told me a story about how he saved the company from collapse three years ago. You all know the story. But do you know who mentored your CEO through those tough times?"

16. "I listened to the news this morning. Apparently, there is no guarantee of job security anywhere. Even if you pay $100,000 to attend a university, there is no guarantee of a job. But there is one trait that people can develop that almost guarantees success. Would you like to know what it is?"

17. "On television this morning, the newscaster announced massive layoffs at our local mega-employer. How will this affect you during the next three months?"

18. "On Facebook this morning, my friend asked me for a donation to his child's school. So would you like to know how to turn down these weekly requests for money, and still keep your friends?"

19. "We just heard the announcement of our exciting new product. But how are you going to turn that into a bestseller, so you can double your commissions?"

20. "When I left Phoenix yesterday afternoon it was hot, like sticking my head inside an oven. But when I got off the plane here in Miami, the humidity made me feel like I was in a sauna. So I wondered, 'Why don't people here in Miami sweat?' Would you like to know what the hotel clerk said?"

21. "Scientists have been doing research into the habits of successful entrepreneurs, and how they can grow million-dollar businesses in less than a year. Would you like to know the results of their survey?"

Starting with a natural conversation with our audience puts them at ease. They won't feel preached to, or talked down to. You are not setting up unrealistic expectations. You are not threatening them and causing them to recoil. Instead, they relax. You are talking with them like you would talk with a friend.

Making our audience engage.

When there is only one answer to our question, the question seems contrived, and it doesn't even need an answer!

We want to make our audience totally focus on the debate in their minds. We want them to focus on what their answer would be to our question.

To make that happen, we need to have them thinking, not about us, but about their own personal experience and how the question affects them.

Asking the audience a series of yes or no questions makes us look manipulative. This causes our audience to lean back in their chairs and question our motives.

By making our questions a bit more complex, our audience will think more deeply about the answers. This is much better than asking simple questions that require only yes or no answers.

Don't make our audience wrong.

When there are multiple answers or opinions to our questions, it allows for everyone in the room to be right. The purpose of our question is not to embarrass the audience, not to prove we have superior intelligence, but to engage their thoughts.

Remember, we want their thoughts on our question and our topic. We don't want them to focus on judging us.

Good questions will build a desire in our audience to gain more knowledge. Now they are very interested in our message.

So are you ready for seven easy starter words that make creating questions easy? Here they are.

Who, What, Which, When, Where, Why, and How.

These words are perfect beginnings to our questions.

We already have a lot of question examples. But try creating some personal examples using these seven words.

More importantly, try saying the questions out loud. When we hear ourselves asking these questions, we can determine if those questions will be comfortable for us.

"Who" questions.

"Who here wants to have the success they've always dreamed of?"

"Who created the rules of social media etiquette?"

"Who would you vote for if all of the current candidates dropped out of the race?"

"Who would you want as your lawyer if you were sued today?"

"Who in this room has the most potential to be successful?"

"Who in this room wants to be financially comfortable in their retirement?"

"Who came here tonight hoping that something in their life would change?"

"Who do we blame the most for our lack of success or happiness?"

"Who is responsible for how we react to our circumstances?"

"Who would you like to be when you grow up?"

"Who is your greatest role model in business/fitness/life?"

"Who will you surprise the most when you become successful?

"Who will be the first person you call when you make enough money to quit your job?"

"Who do you think wants success more: You or the person sitting next to you?"

"Who in this room sacrificed something to be here today?"

"Who here has made sacrifices along the way to get to where you are now?"

"Who wants to stop all that commuting time so you will have more time with your family?"

"Who wants to take a real vacation this year, not just a three-day weekend at your mother-in-law's apartment?"

What is great about "who" questions is that the audience feels you are talking directly with them. This is personal. They love it.

Should we try some "what" questions next?

"What" questions.

Our message is the "what." When we ask a "what" question, our audience is immediately immersed in our message. Our purpose as a speaker is to get the message from our minds to our audience's minds. Our "what" questions help us do that.

Make sure our "what" questions engage the minds of our audience. Here are some examples of "what" questions we could use.

"What is a good first step to start working on a better future?"

"What did you do in life that worked really well?"

"What is the next step for you?"

"What do you want to do with your life?"

"What is the biggest mistake you've made in life, and how are you going to avoid making it again?"

"What is your biggest regret, and do you have time to fix it?"

"What will you do when you retire?"

"What is the first thing you will say to your boss when you quit?"

"What does your ideal day look like?"

"What is your vision of the future?"

"What are your goals for the next three months?"

"What did you do to convince yourself that coming today was a good idea?"

"What are you willing to invest into your good idea? Time, money, energy?"

"What was missing in your last relationship that you will have this time?"

"What worked well in your previous business that you could use in your new venture?"

"What will you say to your family when you have a $10,000 payday?"

"What day of the week is going to be your date night?"

"Which" questions.

Multiple-choice questions are a perfect way to open our speech. It is easy for our audience to make a choice from a few selections that we give them. If we want to be safe, we can give just two alternatives, both of which are acceptable.

This is like a mini-survey. Our audience participates in the safety of their minds. We won't ask them to expose their feelings or preferences. Remember, we want them to like us. We don't want to take our audience out of their comfort zone too quickly.

Some examples of "which" questions:

"Which way do you want to do this project: The hard way or the easy way?"

"Which path did you take after high school: More schooling, or did you immediately look for a job?"

"Which position do you take on making mistakes: Do you want to limit your mistakes, or expand your horizons by making even more mistakes?"

"Which option are you most comfortable with: A short lunch break or a longer lunch break?" (This works well when you are the last speaker before lunch. You bond with your audience because you have read their minds. They are thinking about lunch.)

"Which of these products will attract younger buyers?"

"Which airline would you choose if none of them had frequent flyer programs?"

"Which credit card do you use the most: American Express, MasterCard, or Visa?"

"Which smartphone is better: The iPhone or Samsung? Let me show you proof ..." (The audience immediately takes sides depending on what phone they have. But you challenged them with proof. Now they are going to pay attention for sure.)

Just make sure our "which" questions are topical and relate to our speech. And if our audience immediately chooses sides with their answer, that is okay.

The audience doesn't have to agree with our conclusions, but they do have to be engaged. "Which" questions help them to engage.

39

"When" questions.

This is a question opener that points to a time in the past, present or future. You can get people reflecting, dreaming, or dealing with reality!

Some examples:

"When was the last time you read a book cover-to-cover?"

"When are we going to invest more in education than we do in our prison system?"

"When are you going to make a decision about where you will end your career?"

"When the world is looking for heroes, will you hide?"

"When your family asks when you are going on holiday, what do you tell them?"

"When your spouse looks at you and says this will never work, what will you say?"

"When you don't believe in your own ability to do something, who do you count on to motivate you?"

"When you can't do any more, how do you motivate yourself?"

"When you want to be the one that everyone looks up to, how do you set the example?"

"When it is quitting time at work, how do you really feel about your job?"

"When you know that people are watching, do you act differently?"

"When are you going to decide that you finally deserve success in this career?"

"When will the sight of your credit card statement spur you into budgeting seriously?"

"When your body stops working, will that be the right time to start exercising?"

"When the world is saying to give up, do you listen?"

"When I drove into the carpark today and it was full, what do you think I did to still get here on time?"

"Where" questions.

"Where" questions make our audience think of a place. We transport our audience somewhere else. They forget us and go to a memory, a future goal, or a dream.

Some examples:

"Where were you when they announced the big layoff?"

"Where is the most exciting place in the world for you?"

"Where is the best place in the world to see the sunset?"

"Where is the most amazing seafood in town?"

"Where will the new government take us?"

"Where is the next breakthrough in technology coming from?"

"Where will the children of tomorrow go to get their education?"

"Where do you want to go in this business?"

"Where do you want your investments: In risky stocks, or stable property?"

"Where did you have to be on school nights as a teenager?"

"Where did you go on the weekend when you were a teenager?"

"Where is the one place you never want to go back to?"

"Where did you meet your one true love?"

"Where will you go next if you lose your job tomorrow?"

"Where is the security in today's job market?"

"Why" questions.

When we open with a "why" question, our audience feels free to explore their opinions. A "why" question allows many different viewpoints. We are not looking for absolute answers. Instead, we are exploring possible explanations to why we do things, or why things happen.

One caution. The word "why" has some negative connotations. When we made mistakes, our parents and bosses always asked, "Why did you do that?"

So make sure we don't use "why" to blame the audience for their past. Instead, let's use "why" to help our audience think and to explore new possibilities.

Some examples:

"Why do we feel bad when we watch a sad fictional movie, when we know that these events never happened?"

"Why do some children exhibit anger and throw tantrums in public, yet their siblings do not?"

"Why do we enjoy talking on the phone with our friends, but hate talking to a prospect?"

"Why do we set New Year's goals, and then quit within 48 hours?"

"Why does gum stick to the sidewalk, but not our teeth?"

"Why do we fear public speaking more than death?"

"Why do we crave sweets, but we don't crave sour?"

"Why do we still use plastic bags when paper can be recycled?"

"Why do children push the boundaries during their teenage years, when parents know best?"

"Why do we think working for 40 years is a secure plan, when we know that most people retire broke?"

"Why are we really here tonight?"

"Why is the company outsourcing many of our jobs as I speak?"

"Why do we continue to do the same stupid things, even though they don't work for us?"

"Why" questions are easy and they quickly engage our audience's minds. So when in doubt, use "why" questions to start our speeches and presentations. We will get discussion and interaction. Both reflect well on us, the speaker.

"How" questions.

When we open our speech with a "how" question, our audience expects something new. That is exciting. Everyone loves learning something new that may impact their lives.

Maybe we will explain a secret system or strategy that will make their lives better. Or maybe we will answer a burning question in their minds.

No matter what we ask, our prospects will have to focus on the answer in their heads.

Here are some examples:

"How is it possible to retire from our job in less than five years?"

"How is it possible to fly around the world for less than $3000?"

"How can a normal person build a business part-time, while still working full-time?"

"How did we get into this mess?"

"How is it possible to earn $100,000 a year while working only 10 hours per week?"

"How might a schoolteacher have a greater advantage than a banker in this business?"

"How do young people intuitively know how to work the latest technology?"

"How can we change quickly?"

"How is it possible to build a million-dollar business without an office, staff, or advertising?"

"How can we escape the rat race?"

"How can we use social media to reach our ideal future customers?"

"How can we take the holiday of our dreams, and get someone else to pay for it?"

"How will the result from last night's election affect you?"

"How is it that women can do three things at once, yet men have trouble focusing on a single task?"

"How many days has it been since you exercised? If you need a calendar, that is a bad sign."

"How many days could you survive without a paycheck?"

"How can we lose weight, yet still eat our favorite foods?"

It is easy to engage our audience's instant attention with a "how" question. "How" questions promise a solution, so our audience is sitting on the edges of their seats, waiting to be enlightened.

A caution about rhetorical questions.

During our first 20 seconds, we want people to stop what they are thinking and focus on our question. Rhetorical questions don't engage the mind. They simply make a point.

What is a rhetorical question? Here is an unofficial definition:

A rhetorical question is a question that we ask to highlight our point. It is not a question that we want the audience to verbally answer. In fact, we don't even expect an answer. Rhetorical questions include assumptions about commonly-known facts.

Rhetorical questions can get people to agree with us or acknowledge they understand us.

Here are some examples:

"The emcee has performed well today, hasn't he?"

"Can't you do anything right?"

"Just because your friends jump off a cliff, would you?"

"Do you want to be a loser for the rest of your life?"

"How many times do I have to tell you to pick up your clothes?"

"Does it look like I care?"

"Don't we all want to make more sales?"

Rhetorical questions don't engage the mind. The start of our speech isn't a good place for rhetorical questions. Make sure our opening question engages our listeners' minds, makes them think, and of course, take their minds off us.

Let's review.

Questions are our friends.

Questions take our audience's minds off us, and directs their minds to ponder the question.

Questions involve the audience.

Questions create curiosity.

Questions engage our audience in conversation.

Questions help shy speakers get started.

Asking questions means our audience will stop judging us and get involved with our message.

So relax. Ask an opening question. Take a deep breath for a few seconds to give them a chance to think.

Now, we are starting our speech and our audience loves us.

Shortcut #2: Tell a story.

People love stories. When children are young, one of the things they ask their parents is, "Mommy, Daddy, could you please tell me a story?"

Before the written word, all information was passed on via stories. The human mind is designed to remember stories. That might be good for our speech. We do want our audience to remember our speech, right?

Stories are addictive. This is why we like Hollywood gossip, books, and movies.

Stories engage the mind. When we tell a story, a movie of that story appears inside of our audience's minds.

There is no time to think of anything else. We focus our brain power to project that story on the big-screen television inside of the mind.

Five reasons to start with a story.

1. When we tell a story, we control the thoughts of our audience. Humans are programmed to give instant and full attention to stories.

2. When we tell stories, we won't need notes or ever worry about forgetting what comes next. Stories are the easiest thing to remember.

3. Stories communicate in a non-threatening way. The audience feels safe listening to our story. We are not preaching or telling the audience what to do. People hate being "talked to" but love listening to stories.

4. Facts in stories are more interesting than facts by themselves. Our listeners put themselves inside our story. They see themselves living the facts. This helps us transfer our message to our audience faster.

5. And finally, everyone loves a story. So when we tell stories, our audience will automatically love us.

Sounds like magic, doesn't it?

It is. Audiences will forget the PowerPoint slides and the forced posing by a professional speaker. However, audiences will remember our stories.

At large conferences, the coordinators give speaker surveys to the attendees. The attendees rate the speakers, what they liked, and didn't like. Consistently, the speakers that tell the most stories get the highest marks for being "interesting."

So yes, stories can take control of the thoughts of our audience in the first 20 seconds. The audience gets engaged and loves us. It doesn't get any better than that!

What kind of stories should we tell?

Well, of course the stories should relate to our message. For now, we are only going to talk about an opening story, something that we can use in the first 20 seconds.

Let's break down these story examples into groups. We can refer to these groups later when we prepare our speech.

All stories start with a great opening line, just like the headline of an article in a newspaper, on a blog, or in a magazine.

Want a little fun? You can make our stories as exciting and dramatic as the trashiest tabloid magazine in the world. Tabloids have great headlines, and so should our stories.

Let's look at a few groups of stories.

#1. "When I was young..."

Everyone was young once. Our audience relates immediately. They want to know more about us, and what happened when we were young. Audiences want to relate to the speaker. Let's help them with a short story about us that relates to the message.

If we were talking about health, we could tell about the things we did that affected our health today. Or, we could talk about the healthier, non-processed foods we ate years ago.

If we were talking to someone about a business opportunity, we could talk about our dreams in high school. Young people don't have dreams of working for minimum wage.

If we were presenting boring financial charts and figures to accountants, we could relate how we confuse others with our data.

If we were giving a short speech to toast the groom, we could say how we met the groom in kindergarten.

If we were talking to teachers, we could tell them our feelings when we were in school.

These are interesting stories that anyone can tell. We were there. We simply tell our story. Here is an example.

Saving money.

"When I was young, every week I saw my dad put his pocket change into a big glass jar. It was just pocket change, not much. To me, this hardly seemed worth the effort.

"Then, when I graduated from high school, reality hit me. When I applied to university, they insisted on huge tuition fees. This certainly wasn't like the free ride I got in high school. When I turned to my dad for help, he said, 'I have been saving pocket change for your future for 18 years. Here is the money you need to get you through your first two years of university.'"

Skin care.

"When I was young, I loved the sun. I loved having a year-round tan. When I couldn't sunbathe, I bought time at the local tanning salon.

"Now, just 30 years later, I have wrinkles so deep I could hide small bottles of anti-aging cream in them. I ruined my skin for life. I didn't know what you know today."

Got the idea? Our audience wants to know what happened to us when we were young. They know it will be interesting because we will relate it to the message that we will deliver.

Let's look at another group of stories.

#2. "Last night I..."

The fact that what happened is so recent is compelling, because it's about as fresh as a story can get. If we knew what the latest Hollywood star was doing last night, before any of our friends, we would be getting all the attention for sharing it.

Our audience is the same. Tell them what happened last night and we invite them into our world and our experiences. If what happened last night has a lesson that relates to our speech, even better.

Here are some examples.

Buffalo, NY.

"Last night I landed here in Buffalo during your normal five months of blizzards. Took me three hours by snowplow just to get to this hotel. But when I arrived at this hotel, everyone was friendly and smiling. I thought to myself, 'Why?' It is dark, it is late, and it is freezing. Travel is almost impossible. But everyone is smiling!

"So I asked the check-in clerk, 'Hey! Why is everyone so happy?'

"The clerk replied, 'Well, there are only three more months of dark and blizzards to go before our two weeks of summer!'

"Wow! What a great attitude. And every staff member I met at this hotel had that same great outlook on life.

"So it is not what happens to us in life, it is how we react that counts. Nowhere else in the world is this more true than right here in Buffalo.

"Now, how was your attitude when you woke up this morning?"

Best man speech.

"Last night the groom and I went out for a drink at our favorite hangout. This would be the last time we would be having drinks together as single, uncommitted guys, just looking to have fun. After our final drink, the groom turned to me and said, 'You know, I am not going to miss you and this bar. I am excited about my new life starting tomorrow. Instead of drifting through life looking for a few laughs, I will now be building a future with the woman of my dreams. Sorry to break the news to you, buddy, but you need to get a life just like mine.'"

Business opportunity meeting.

"Last night I talked to my brother. He was devastated. His boss came up to him yesterday and said, 'I don't know how we would get along without you, but starting this afternoon, we are going to try.'

"No notice. No warning. No tissue for the tears that ran down my brother's cheeks. My brother realized he had failed to plan for better security for his family. He knows he should have started his part-time business a year ago. Now, he is struggling with depression, denial, and wondering how to get a few dollars for this month's car payments."

Finding prospects.

"Last night I ate at your semi-famous Bread Buffet. When I paid my bill, the chatty clerk told me about her daughter entering college, but without enough money for books and food. The clerk said, 'I wish I knew five years ago how to save a bit of money every month. Then my daughter would have that money now for books and food. But, I just didn't know how.'

"My thoughts? There are thousands of people here in the community just like that clerk who desperately need your financial planning help. Stop keeping it a secret. People need you!

"So here is how I would get the word out about your services..."

Dieting.

"Last night I ate two slices of cheesecake, and a full helping of frozen tiramisu. Yes, that was bad for my diet. But, I have a secret.

"One bad meal every so often won't make you fat. If you have reasonable discipline on most meals, weight management isn't a problem. So don't go on thinking you have to starve yourself for life.

"Write down three of your favorite foods that you miss right now in your notes. Then I will show you when you can eat them."

Ready for some more story openings?

#3. "During the break I was talking to..."

During the coffee break, most attendees have a coffee, talk about the weather, the sports results, and how their families are doing. If we talk about something interesting that happened during the break, we will grab our audience's attention. If our story is about someone who is in the audience, it will make that person feel special. Of course, we would make sure to get permission to use the story from the person we will highlight. Here is an example.

Teacher's conference.

"During the break I was talking to Mary Smith, your principal. She told me, 'Mark, this is a tough school district. Our teachers should get combat pay, but we just can't afford it. What can we do to improve their working conditions in the classroom?'"

At this point, every teacher in the audience is nodding with agreement. They feel we share a common concern with them. Our audience is giving us their full attention.

Sales conference.

"During the break, I was talking to Joe Jones, your sales manager. He told me, 'Mark, sales are down. 20% of the people attending this conference will be gone in two months unless we turn sales around quickly. What can we do to get more leads for our salesmen?'"

Now, every salesman in the room is looking around. Who will be in the 20% that has to go if sales don't improve? Ah, but there is a promise by the speaker. Maybe the speaker will tell us how to get more leads.

The audience isn't thinking about us or judging us. They are focused on their survival. They don't want to be in the 20% that may lose their jobs in two months.

Do we have their attention? Of course.

Humor.

If we feel comfortable with humor, we could adjust the "During the break..." story to make a little fun of ourselves. Humor, by definition, is making fun of someone. Make sure we are making fun of ourselves, not the audience. Here is an example.

"During the break, I heard three people chatting about this conference. One of them said, 'If I see one more speaker with a white shirt, red tie, and dark suit, I am just going to vomit.' So I am thinking, 'Ouch. I made a poor choice of wardrobe today. But I might as well wear my white shirt, red tie, and dark suit. My only other choice is coming up here in my underwear, and that would make the majority of the room ill.'"

Okay, that is a stretch. Not for beginners. But remember, if we are comfortable with humor, it is just another way to get the audience to stop judging us, and have a good laugh.

#4. "When I woke up this morning..."

Everyone in our audience woke up this morning. That's pretty normal.

So what happened to us might be interesting. Want a quick example?

Evil.

"When I woke up this morning, I had a strange feeling that something was different, and very, very wrong. Sort of a deep, dark, sinister feeling that something evil had happened. When I opened the curtains of my bedroom, I saw the evil. Yes, it was a bright, sunny, perfect day for golfing. And, all of us are stuck here inside of the hotel for a conference on happiness."

Remember, we just want to distract the audience's minds, and direct their attention to the message we will deliver. We don't want our audience to sit back, fold their arms, and judge us.

One more example?

Exercise.

"When I woke up this morning, I remembered that there are 'morning' people and 'evening' people. Well, the evening people were still sleeping, getting rest, so that their body can function better during the day. But not me. I am a 'morning' person. I decided to go jogging in the freezing rain, deeply inhaling the fumes from the automobiles of the commuters, fighting off rabid dogs defending their owner's homes, sliding on the slippery sidewalks, and scraping my knees. All this, just so that I can tell those stupid 'evening' people, 'Hey, look at me. I am healthy!'"

#5. "In the future..."

We all want to know the future. Some people even pay fortunetellers to predict what will happen in their lives. The future is interesting. Let's try this example.

Schools of the future.

"In the future, schools will have armed guards at the entrances to the classrooms. Metal detectors will check children for guns when they enter the school property. Chain link fences will seal the children in, and keep outsiders away. Oh wait, that's already happening. We are the future of schools. So how did we get to this sad situation when all we wanted to do was educate our children?"

Town hall meeting.

"In the future, we won't have to get babysitters while we come to our monthly town hall meeting. Instead, we will have the issues posted on the Internet for us to study. We will vote or comment from the comfort of our homes.

"But this future won't come unless we approve high-speed Internet access to every home in our community. And here are the five best reasons that we should vote 'Yes' on this evening's issue."

Work.

"In the future, the four-day work week will be the norm. That means we will have three full days to fight with our family, lie on the couch watching meaningless drama on our televisions, develop carpel tunnel syndrome from surfing the Internet, and slowly allow our lives to drift towards death.

"Not exactly a pretty picture. But, we can change that future now by taking these three steps towards personal growth and a meaningful life."

Food.

"In the future, our entire three meals a day will shrink into this one little pill. One pill, all the nutrition we need. Yes, we will miss the aroma and taste sensations of eating real food. We will miss dinner conversations with people we love. No need for teeth or fast food restaurants. But change brings new opportunities. Would you like to take a peek at what that future will look like for your children and grandchildren?"

Book.

"When I woke up this morning, I reached over and grabbed my book of motivational quotes. I flicked the pages, and here is what I read. 'Every day, someone wins a lottery. Unfortunately, that 'someone' isn't you.' And then, things got worse as my morning progressed..."

Okay, let's move on to another type of story to start our presentations.

Fictional stories.

Sometimes we have to make up a story to deliver the right message. That is okay. Not every message you will deliver in a speech has a ready-made real-life story that you can use. Want some examples?

"Once upon a time..."

Oh, my. Have we heard that opening before? That opening has been used for centuries. We love this opening. It takes us back to our childhood memories of listening to fairy tales. Everyone in our audience will have good feelings as their minds imagine the details of our story.

The "once upon a time" opening signals that a story has begun. But this is a fictional story. What will we do next?

No worries. Stories have a predictable pattern. When we create a fictional story, here is one template we could use:

A. "Once upon a time..."

B. "And everyday life was this way..."

C. "But then, one day (something happens)..."

D. "Now (every day is different)..."

E. "And because of this we learned..."

Let's put this to work. Imagine we are giving a lecture to teachers and our message is to allow children to be themselves, to be creative, and to see what their natural talent could be. We decide to start our speech with this fictional story.

The story of Michael.

"Once upon a time, there was a hyperactive child named Michael. Every day he twisted and turned at his desk, tapped his fingers, squirmed and couldn't sit still. But then one day, the teacher introduced a dance exercise in her class. Michael flew across the room, moonwalked, did the happy dance, and stunned the entire class with his energy and moves. Now, every day the teacher starts her class with one minute of dancing. The children love it. And Michael gets to express himself. He then sits attentively through the rest of the class. And because of this we learned that if we allow children just a single minute to express themselves, they will be more attentive when we teach their lessons."

Is this the story of Michael Jackson? No, it isn't. This is a fictional story! But wouldn't that be a great ending to prove that by allowing children to be different, some incredible talents might emerge?

Let's do another example of this story format.

In this example, imagine we are selling a business opportunity to people who have boring 9-to-5 jobs. We create this fictional story.

Boring jobs.

"Once upon a time, there was a discouraged employee named Joe. Every day Joe woke up to his screaming alarm clock, crawled out of bed, holding his head from not getting enough sleep. But then one day, Joe said, 'Enough! I am going to start my own business and wake up every morning when I am done sleeping!' Now, every day Joe wakes up happy. He is his own boss. And he commutes only five minutes from his home and family. And because Joe became his own boss, he is building **his** dream, not the dream of his former boss."

But what if we sold a magical protein diet shake? Let's try this.

The "fat aunt."

"Once upon a time, there was a sad woman named Mary, who struggled to lose weight. Her family was cruel. Even her nieces called her the 'fat aunt.' Every day Mary would try a new weight-loss fad diet or exercise, and then get discouraged at the end of the day. But then, one day, Mary met her old friend Joyce. Joyce said, 'Mary, stop dieting. Even if dieting worked, as soon as you stop dieting, the weight will come back. Instead, just drink this low-calorie protein shake for breakfast. It tastes good, and it has fewer calories than donuts. The weight will fall off effortlessly.' Now, every day Mary simply has her protein shake for breakfast. She never thinks about dieting. Her weight adjusts naturally. And because of this change, Mary's younger sister is now known as the 'fat aunt.'"

Okay, one more. Imagine we gave a speech to our class reunion. And maybe this isn't so fictional. Let's try this.

The class reunion.

"Once upon a time, a group of students became the best friends anyone could imagine. Every day they attended class, sporting events and parties, and vowed to be best friends forever. But then one day, they graduated. Some students went to far-away universities. Some started their own families in different cities. And soon, they lost touch with their best friends. Now, these friends became lonely. They wanted to share their lives with their friends from the past. They realized life is measured by the happiness we get from our friends. And because of this, we organized this 20th year class reunion. Now we can connect again, and be the best friends forever that we vowed to be 20 years ago."

Is this the only fictional story template?

Of course not. This is just a simple template to get us started in creating our fictional story.

The point is, fictional stories can work. Our audience will listen. They want to know what comes next. And they forget about judging us.

Movie stories.

Movies transport the viewers to a different place and time. Our minds enjoy the transporting experience. This kind of story is a great way to start a speech.

Pick a popular movie that most of our audience is familiar with. Choose a scene or dialog from that movie to start our speech. Why?

If our audience liked the movie, they immediately recalled seeing the movie. And how did they feel? Great. Now our audience has a good feeling about us.

This opening triggers memories, feelings, and emotions. They focus on the movie, not us.

Many famous movies have memorable dialog or scenes we can refer to. Just pick a movie genre that seems to match our audience. Some audiences will relate well to action and adventure. Other audiences will love romance or comedy.

Let's see how we can open with our flashback to a movie.

"You had me at 'Hello.'"

Let's say our speech was to motivate salespeople to make more sales calls. We want to impress upon them that if they had more contacts, they would naturally find some prospects ready to buy. So, we could start our speech by saying:

"In the movie *Jerry Maguire*, Tom Cruise comes back to the woman he loves and babbles on mindlessly asking for forgiveness. She interrupts him by saying, 'You had me at... hello.'"

We could use this dialog to grab their attention and put the audience in a great mood. This would illustrate our message that if we see enough prospects, some prospects will buy just because we are there.

"If I can change and you can change, everybody can change."

If we spoke to new employees, we could start our speech by saying:

"In the movie *License to Wed*, Robin Williams plays Reverend Frank. Reverend Frank insists that Ben and Sadie go through his marriage prep course. They write their own vows. Then he also demands chastity, bugs their apartment, initiates arguments, and tests them in the least romantic way. So today, welcome to the orientation to your career at Mega Corporation."

"It ain't how hard you hit..."

If we were giving a talk about going for our goals, we could reference the one and only Rocky Balboa. He makes a point that multiple failures and mistakes can be overcome. We could start by quoting Rocky.

"In the movie *Rocky Balboa*, Rocky says, 'It ain't about how hard you hit. It's about how hard you can get hit and keep moving forward; how much you can take and keep moving forward.'"

Now we can move forward, inspiring audience members that have let past failures stop their progress.

"Perfection."

If we want to tell our audience that success comes through a systematic and methodical approach, we could say this:

"Denzel Washington played Coach Herman Boone in *Remember the Titans*. He told the team, 'We will be perfect in every aspect of the game. You drop a pass, you run a mile. You miss a blocking assignment, you run a mile. You fumble the football, and I will break my foot off in your John Brown hindparts, and then you will run a mile. Perfection. Let's go to work.'"

"Regret."

If we want to remind an audience that doing their best is okay, then we could start by saying:

"Liam Neeson plays the German businessman Oskar Schindler in *Schindler's List*. He manages to save people from the Nazi extermination camps. In his closing statements, he is afraid he hasn't done enough. He says, 'I could have got more out. I could have got more. I don't know. If I'd just... I could have got more.' His co-star says to him, 'Oskar, there are eleven hundred people who are alive because of you. Look at them.'"

"Challenges."

If you want to start a talk by referring to the challenges facing the wives of returning war veterans, you might reference Chris Kyle's wife in *American Sniper*.

"You are my husband, you are the father of my children. Even when you are here, you are not here. I see you, I feel you, but you are not here."

"They are not going to dial themselves!"

Prospecting secrets from *The Wolf of Wall Street*.

"Leonardo di Caprio has a great line to inspire action in his sales team. 'See those little black boxes? They are called telephones. I am gonna let you in on a little secret about those telephones. They are not going to dial themselves. Okay?'"

"It happened again."

Want to remind people that lightning can strike twice? That history will repeat itself if we don't change anything about our behavior or environment?

"In *The Hangover Part II*, the movie opens in a Bangkok hotel room, with the fan slowly turning. The stars wake up with hangovers, shaved heads, and tattoos. They spend the first 15 minutes in a daze discovering more and more disturbing facts. Then Bradley Cooper has to make the dreaded call to his wife... 'It happened again.'"

This joke makes more sense to people who saw the first *Hangover* movie. We have to be familiar with our audience.

Imagine if we started our speech with, "Ladies and gentlemen, it happened again."

Instantly, everyone in the audience is wondering, "What happened?" We have the audience's curiosity and attention.

"I want it to mean something."

You don't have to have a big budget to beat the big boys.

"Brad Pitt won critical acclaim in the movie *Moneyball*. He tried to put a competitive team together with a low budget. He explains to us that making a difference is possible and that we can change the world. He says, 'But if we win, on our budget, with this team... we will have changed the game. And that is what I want. I want it to mean something.'"

If we are talking to a group, this "underdog" approach is easy for the group to identify with. They feel that we are part of their team. It is a great feeling when the audience is on our side.

When the audience needs motivation.

One of the greatest athletes of all time? Muhammad Ali. Will Smith plays Ali in the movie of the same name. Will shows us the challenges, the struggles, and the victories of an athlete who would not back down from his beliefs. During Ali's prime, every schoolboy pretending to be a boxer knew this quote:

"Float like a butterfly, sting like a bee. His hands can't hit what his eyes can't see."

A great quote to start our speech. Then we could ask a question like, "Remember Muhammad Ali? He too was an underdog going into his first championship fight. Yet he showed confidence in the face of fear. What scares us most in life?"

"Be unique."

Sometimes we want to relate to an audience that considers themselves "outsiders" or "unique." You can get their approval by acknowledging that being different is okay.

"Benedict Cumberbatch played the nerdiest nerd in the movie *The Imitation Game*. He was trying to break the secret code that the Germans used in the war. At the end of the movie, his co-star reminds him of the impact his work had. She says:

"'Do you know, this morning I was on a train that went through a city that wouldn't exist if it wasn't for you. I bought a ticket from a man who would likely be dead if it wasn't for you. I read up on my work, a whole field of scientific inquiry that only exists because of you. Now, if you wish you could have been normal... I can promise you I do not. The world is an infinitely better place precisely because you weren't.'"

"Supersize me."

"Sugar will make you fat. It has to be a true fact because it is in a movie!

"Morgan Spurlock went 30 days eating only at McDonald's in *Supersize Me*. He said he would order regular sizes, but accept all Supersize offers if they were made to him. In the results, he makes a shocking confession. Every health advocate in the world loves to quote him when they talk about the evils of sugar.

"'I consumed thirty pounds of sugar from their food. That's a pound a day.'"

Now, if we started our speech by talking about the evils of fast food or sugar, wouldn't it be great to have a one-pound bag of sugar as a prop?

Enough movie examples to spur our creative thinking? Let's move on to more story ideas.

More story ideas using other people.

Remember, everyone is hard-wired to want to hear stories. As long as our stories are interesting and have a point, we will find the start of our presentations easy. Let's look at more ways to open with stories.

Stories about other people.

Our audience wants to know what is happening in the lives of others. If our story has a twist, instead of a predictable ending, our audience will be amused. For now, let's start with a guaranteed way to engage our audience's imagination.

Our mother.

Everyone has a mother. Everyone relates. Our mothers told us something wise, or maybe did something that taught us a lesson. When we start with our mother, the audience will lean forward.

Some examples.

"My mother was a strong woman. When service people tried to cheat her or charge more money, she would scold them and threaten to call their mother! We should not fear standing up for what we believe is right."

71

"My mother was strict. If we didn't clean our rooms, we didn't get food. Mothers are where we get our initial values in life. What about your mother? Was she the first person to give you values for your life?"

"My mother always said, 'Don't judge people by what they say, only judge people by what they do.' And as salesmen, we can promise the sales manager that big things are coming; but if we don't produce, we don't get paid."

"When I was seven years old, my mother did something incredible..."

"When I was eight years old, my mother got me a dog. Not just any dog. She got me a St. Bernard that was twice my size. Then, she gave me a leash to take the dog for a walk. Well, you know what happened next..."

"My mother was a selfless woman. Every day she would make our lunches, drive us to school and then volunteer to help other people. When I went to university, she even let me take the car while she rode her bike to work. I can never be grateful enough to my mother."

"My mother has always been a great friend to me. I have never stopped having conversations with her about the things that are important to me. I will never stop listening to her advice. This sort of relationship is what we all dream of and can nurture in our lives."

Our father.

"My father used to spend a lot of time in front of radios. Ham radios, those ancient radios that used Morse code, any type of radio. His love of electronics, radios, and machines helped him get into computers in the 1970s. This gave him a career that made every day special. He loved going to work. So do you have a job that makes you feel this way?"

Or, how about this example?

"My father loved sports. He played tennis two or three times a week, and helped me with my competitive personality. Just as important though, was how my father taught me to take responsibility. Whether I won or lost, I was never allowed to blame the conditions or other people. So yes, the economy is bad, but we must be bigger than that problem."

Our uncle.

"Black sheep" create interesting stories. Maybe the uncle fled the country or lost a lot of money. People love to hear about rebels, entrepreneurs, and tales of drunken parties with the eccentric uncle as the lead character.

"My Uncle Jim sold vacuum cleaners. He drank, smoked, and did outrageous things to sell vacuum cleaners. More than once he told ridiculous lies just to get a sale. While we all love eccentric uncles, we don't want to lie to meet our sales quotas. So let's look at how we can sell more while still being ethical."

Our boss.

We all have at least one story about our boss.

"My first boss was a cocaine addict that had lost all his short-term memory. Every day I went to his office and asked him, 'Where is that raise you promised me yesterday?' In just two years I became the highest-paid employee in the company. Yes, if you don't ask, you won't get what you want."

Our high school teacher.

"Mrs. Longworth was my high school history teacher. She knew I had trouble reading. Rather than give up on me, she encouraged me to watch the History Channel every day. I loved it. I became addicted to history. And because of her, I can stand before you as a fully-qualified high school graduate. So, what holds you back? And how can we get past our hurdles in life?"

So let's use our imagination. We can have stories about the waitress, the taxi driver, the banker, the circus clown, and even weird co-workers. People provide great stories. We just have to pay attention.

Current event stories.

"Right now..." is the perfect opening for current event stories. With 24-hour news programs, it is easy to find a story to fit our needs as the speaker. Let's look at a few examples.

"Right now in New York City, someone is getting mugged. Why? Because someone else needs money to live. When our social welfare programs fail, crime increases. The need to survive exceeds the need to obey society's laws. So what can we do to reduce the number of disadvantaged people in our cities?"

"Right now, one out of three people in this room is quietly racing towards a heart attack. Look to the person on the left. Look to the person on the right. If both of them look healthy... then you should worry. So how do we know when a heart attack is imminent?"

"Right now, anyone earning minimum wage can't afford to live in our city. Yesterday a cashier told me, 'I have to commute two hours every day, just to earn minimum wage. I don't know how to change my life.' Well, that is why we are here today. We want to reach these people and change their lives."

"Right now, everyone is talking about the World Championships. Why are we worried about overpaid players that we don't know? Why aren't we more worried about the pollution around our schools? Do we value sports more than our children?"

"Right now, our mayor is laughing himself silly with all his corruption money stored safely in the bank he owns. Why do we let this happen? Why do we elect him term after term? Are we so apathetic that we deserve to have our tax money stolen?"

Now, the more controversial our opening is, the more our audience gets involved. Conflict is interesting. No one wants to hear a boring story. People want to take sides in an argument.

Be careful, though. If we are new, or unprepared, we don't want to start a riot in our audience.

Just remember that conflict forces people to focus on the words we say. Our audience loves to hear the news, especially with an opinion.

More current event openings.

Here are 30 opening phrases that will help us tell a current event story to our audience.

* On the red carpet in Los Angeles...

* The latest Versace collection in Milan...

* With the recent opening of the Grand Hotel...

* After the big hurricane here in Miami...

* Seeing the daredevil jump off the Golden Gate Bridge, many people thought...

* Last week in the Moscow subway...

* Our treasured beaches turned brown last night...

* Last weekend's blizzard taught us...

* After the death of Princess Diana, we all felt...

* Income taxes are due tomorrow. So why are we here delaying filling out our forms for another day?

* Let's stick our heads inside a closed garage with a running car. That is the current level of air pollution in....

* With the recent increase in bank fees, you and I are actually losing money when we use our banks. Let me show you...

* The latest research shows that the healthiest and safest place to live... isn't here. So why do we stay in this city...

* The biggest robbery in the history of the world just happened. The thieves didn't wear masks. Instead, they disguised themselves as elected officials of our country...

* Ten years ago today, this silent tragedy happened...

By mentioning a current event, our audience will focus on our message. This is not the only way to tell a story, but it is definitely an effective way.

Enough about stories, let's get on to Shortcut #3.

Shortcut #3: Exercises.

Want to take the audience's minds from judging us... to somewhere else?

Easy.

Immediately involve the audience in an exercise. Now they will focus on the exercise. Pre-judging us is a long-lost thought.

Here are some examples of exercises we can use to start our presentations.

Easy writing exercises.

At conferences, most people will have paper and pens. Wedding receptions? Probably not.

Let's get our audience immediately taking notes. This isn't a pushy command. Our audience complies with our request as they think this will be important.

#1: Ask our audience to write a simple answer to a simple question.

Our audience has to concentrate on completing this task. Maybe we can say, "Write down the first thing you do after brushing your teeth in the morning."

Lots of thoughts are going through our audience's heads. They might be thinking:

* "I wonder what my friend, Joe, is going to write down."

* "Oh, this is going to be interesting. I wonder what this will have to do with today's topic."

* "Gosh, I am not sure. Let me think back to this morning."

Their minds are engaged. While they are writing, we take a deep breath to help us relax. Then we can continue with the topic associated with what our audience wrote down. Because the question is simple, most people will participate. They won't fear being wrong or feeling embarrassed.

#2. Ask them to write down a short list or group of items.

People love to fill out lists, quizzes, and small tests. It helps them prove to themselves how smart they are. We will make this seem simple to our audience by letting them know the list will be short.

A list of three things is simple enough for most people. Long lists can be a challenge. Don't ask the audience to make a list of 20. This will take too long. Few will complete it. The dead silence of the audience will kill the opening to our speech.

Even a list of 10 things can seem too difficult. Stick with just asking for a maximum of three things. Later, after our speech is in progress, we can read a "Top Ten" list of examples. This gives us more time to engage and bond with our audience.

Some examples.

"Write down the three most fattening foods you can think of."

"Write down the two biggest problems with your health."

"Write down the one word that describes your mother-in-law."

When the audience writes things down, it makes their lists real and concrete. This gives the audience something to focus on for the next few minutes of our talk. Plus, the audience is already taking notes. They are engaged.

This is a great ice breaker with our audience also. Surprising them with something funny makes us more likable. This is another way to bond with the audience and build trust so that later we can introduce more serious and important issues.

Let's continue with some more examples.

#3. "Write down three things you would do if you had an extra $10,000."

People dream of luxuries and retirement. However, most wish to pay off their mortgage, credit card bills, and maybe take a vacation. Having just three things on this list gets the activity finished in about 15 or 20 seconds. Then we can share the results to make the audience feel they are part of the conversation. We can ask, "By a show of hands, how many people had 'paying off debt' on your list? By a show of hands, how many people had a vacation on their list?"

Now we are having a conversation with our audience instead of preaching to them. They are involved, and have long forgotten about judging us.

#4. "Write down where you would be right now, if you never had to show up for work again."

Most people will put their ultimate travel destination, sports team stadium, and some will want to be at home watching television. This will bring a moment of euphoria to the audience. And then, a dip of depression. They realize they still have to show up for work unless something changes. Hopefully our speech will reveal options for them. They want us to show them how.

#5. "Write down the one problem in your business that you would like to solve today."

Your audience of business owners might write: more customers, staffing, bills, money or advertising. They have to choose just one. When we know which one it is, we can adjust our speech to their most popular problem... if we are prepared.

So let's concentrate our talk on one problem and the solution. Trying to do three topics in one talk is just too challenging and confusing. We want to invest our first 20 seconds bonding with our audience. Then we can serve their needs with the rest of our speech.

#6. "Write down one sentence that explains to your kids what you do for a living."

This is a great opening for a speech on simplifying our communication skills. We can prime our audience by giving them examples. Here is a good chance to add a little humor if that fits our personality. We would ask them to write a simple sentence such as:

* I am a teacher.

* I am a carpenter.

* I am a stunt double for James Bond.

* I run the copy machine in a big office.

* I drive a taxi and get to talk to interesting people all day.

* I babysit a 49-year-old boss who can't do anything for himself.

Now, watch what happens. The audience is thinking hard about how they will describe what they do in one sentence. Again, they forget about judging us. Their focus is on their sentence.

We can get more interaction by asking the audience, "Who wrote down the longest sentence? The shortest sentence?"

We can get a few examples from the audience. Many times someone will have a corporate-speak answer that they would give their colleagues. It sounds something like this:

"I am the corporate liaison that interfaces with human resources to effect the regulatory directives within the realm of labor law."

We could mention to the audience, "Wow. This person must have really intelligent kids!"

Or, a teacher might say, "I facilitate the academic development of future leaders with emotional and mental support."

We will get a few examples of confusing jargon to establish the description problem with our audience. The key is that our audience is involved.

#7. "Write down the first words you would say if the cashier told you, 'This credit card has been declined.'"

If we wanted to add a little humor, say, "And your answer has to be more than four letters."

Our audience now drifts back into their minds to see if that ever happened to them. And if it didn't happen to them, they imagine what they would say. Keeping the audience's minds busy is what we want to do.

This is a good opening for a talk on stress or confrontation. This would tell our audience that we understand how they feel.

#8. "With one word, write down the feeling you have when you wake up in the morning and think about work. No profanity, please."

This is a great exercise to share with the room. Some people love their work. They like the routine and habits work gives them. Others feel sick to their stomach. Now our presentation can continue with finding the ideal career, or changing our attitude towards our work. Expect a few giggles in the room as people make jokes and look at each other's words.

#9. "If you wanted to write a book, write down a title for that book now."

Many people dream of becoming authors. Research in the United Kingdom last year showed that becoming a writer was the #1 desired career.

People think writing is a romantic profession. They picture themselves sitting at their computer, emptying their thoughts and feelings, writing epic novels and memoirs. For some, writing is creative. If this is an appropriate audience, most will already have an idea for a book in their heads.

So if we are talking to potential authors, this would be a nice opening. Our speech might cover procrastination or setting writing goals.

#10. Write down the one great quote you use to motivate yourself when you want to procrastinate.

Depending on our audience, most people won't have a quote. High school students probably don't pick quotes to remember. Other audiences may have spent their lives with negative people. So sometimes we might have to give our example first. In this case, we might prime our audience by telling them, "Whenever I don't want to do a task, I say this out loud, 'If not now, then when?' And that usually gets me to decide to start the task right away."

#11. "Write down the title of your favorite personal development book."

Then, we should give a few examples of some book titles to help them come up with their answer. Some groups don't read personal development books, so again, we might have to prime them with some examples.

#12. The power of three.

The "power of three" has been around for a long time. We love to have choices. For example, we could have a choice of pricing. Cheap, mid-range, and expensive. People seem to remember things in groups of three better. No explanation for this phenomenon. People just like things in threes.

Let's ask our audience some "three" questions to get them involved. For example:

* "List three bad habits you would like to get rid of."

Getting these on paper is confronting the issue. This can lead to a discussion about judgements, values, self-esteem, etc. Also, this provides a goal to achieve. Now, it is up to us to help them quit these habits in our speech. We started with a promise, so we better have some good advice.

* "Write down three countries you would like to visit."

The key here is in the wanting, not the number. We get the audience dreaming. Now we can talk about why people pick certain countries. Maybe it is safety, romance, panoramic views, or the culture.

* "Write down three of your favorite foods that make you fat."

Some in our audience will have to put down their donuts to write their answers. People love to write about their favorite foods. If we were talking about dieting, we might interest the audience by showing them how they can eat those foods and still lose weight. Or, a way of balancing other foods to reduce their calorie intake.

* "Entrepreneurs... are different. Write down three things you think entrepreneurs do differently than other people."

This works equally well with an audience of entrepreneurs, or an audience of career jobholders. Both groups can think of three things entrepreneurs do differently. If the audience is small, you could ask them to shout out the weirdest things so others might add them to their list.

* "Write down these three numbers in a private place. Don't let anyone see your numbers."

Wow. Mystery, curiosity, intrigue. Our audience is wondering what comes next. They are sitting on the edge of their chairs. If these numbers have to be secret, why?

Some examples of numbers you could ask for:

1. How much money you earn per month.

2. How much money you have in the bank.

3. How much credit card debt and other debt you have.

Or, we could ask for these three numbers:

1. Your weight.

2. Your height.

3. The number of donuts you eat per week.

Or:

1. Your age.

2. The age of your first memories.

3. How many years before you retire.

Or:

1. The number of weeks you work for your boss.

2. The number of weeks you have for yourself.

3. The number of family holidays you take every year.

Or,

1. The number of cars in the driveway.

2. The number of cellphones in the family.

3. The number of family vacations taken in the last year.

Thinking in threes is fun. Just create a little quiz that is relevant to our speech. While the audience fills out their list of threes, you can have a sip of water, adjust your microphone, look for the nearest exit, see how the audience is responding, and relax a bit.

#13. "One to Ten" ideas.

Having a range or scale is useful because it is individualized. Our audience will place themselves into the picture we create. This is more specific than yes or no. It allows for shades of grey. The audience has to forget about judging us, and concentrate on what number they will choose. Here are some examples.

* "On a scale of one to ten, with ten being the best possible outcome, write down a rating of your success in life."

Now this will take some thinking and evaluating. Most people are doing better than they think. They might have achieved a lot of success in their lives. Many people in our audience will understate their success.

It is not easy to evaluate our success until we see a comparison. For example, someone who feels unsuccessful might change his mind when he learns that millions of people around the world earn less than $5 a day. Maybe our speech addresses our self-confidence and self-image.

What happens if you get an inflated ego audience member who claims to be a 10-out-of-10 super-success? Easy.

Refer to that person in our presentation as an example to inspire others. The egomaniac will feel honored, and the rest of our audience can get on with our talk.

* "On a scale of one to ten, write down how happy you are."

Happiness of others depends on a lot of issues beyond our control. But we can be in charge of our happiness score. Everyone wants to be happier. We have the audience's attention. They are excited to hear new solutions to their lack of happiness.

What should we do if we notice that half of our audience is depressed?

Let them know we will have a solution. Now they are excited to hear what we have to say. They are going to love us. We can be the light at the end of the tunnel that gives them hope.

* "On a scale of one to ten, write down your success as a businessperson."

This question gets our audience looking inward. Now they are judging themselves, not us. When our audience realizes they have room to grow and develop, they feel more coachable and will listen to us with an open mind. We can't judge them, but they can (and will) judge themselves.

* "On a scale of one to ten, write down your confidence level for public speaking."

Watch the audience closely. Some members will move their chairs to the back of the room! That is a hint. We don't want to call on or ask these people a question during our speech.

Other audience members will grade themselves as an "8" or a "10" in confidence. So if we want a volunteer, make sure to pick one of these people. We don't want to embarrass shy people during our speech. We want to create fans for our message, not enemies.

What happens if everyone in the room looks down at their paper, and no one is giving us eye contact? Huge hint. Make sure we don't take our audience members out of their comfort zone with exercises and audience participation. Asking this audience to raise their hands might be too confronting! We want our audience to listen in a safe environment.

Physical exercises.

Physical exercises definitely get the audience involved. Movement creates excitement. Let's look at some physical exercises we could use to start our speech.

#1. "Please shake hands with the person sitting next to you, but use your left hand instead of your right."

When they finish, we could describe the different types of handshakes, and what they tell you about that person. Everyone is looking forward to what that would mean to them.

Speaker Bernie De Souza from the United Kingdom starts many of his speeches by asking people to shake hands with someone near them. He then demonstrates how, using a slight turning motion, we can detect if our partner will be more open or more resistant to new ideas. After the demonstration, the partners try it again with their focus on their new skill.

#2. "Please stand up, bend over and see if you can touch your toes."

The audience loves involvement and action. They want to know what we are going to say because many of them can't quite touch their toes!

This activity requires that the audience get out of their chairs. Movement creates excitement. Wouldn't we want an excited audience?

Now, this exercise is going to look pretty stupid if we don't tie it in with our topic. So make sure this exercise, or any exercise, complements our topic.

#3. "Turn to the person next to you. Let's test your logic. See how many questions you have to ask to guess your partner's middle name. Remember to keep count!"

A great opening exercise to get our audience talking. There is nothing worse than an audience that sits back, folds their arms, and gives us the look of scorn. The look that says, "Okay, tell me something I don't already know, and it better be good!" That look makes even the most seasoned speaker sweat.

Now, what will happen? Some people will cheat. They will ask the question, "What is your middle name?" Some will start guessing what the first letter of the middle name is. And yes, some will just feel out of their comfort zone and talk about something else. It is okay. We got our audience involved.

What kind of follow-up could we have to this question? We could then continue by saying:

1. If you guessed your partner's middle name in less than five questions, you have a high "logic IQ" and are good at solving puzzles.

2. If you took more than ten questions and still couldn't guess your partner's middle name, please don't apply for entry into MENSA.

3. If you cheated, and just asked your partner, "Hey, what is your middle name?"... Well, I am scared to play games with you, because obviously you know how to find shortcuts to win.

4. If you didn't participate at all, maybe thought this was silly, then it tells me that you only focus on serious matters that mean something in your life. (Yes, even the skeptics who didn't like us have to start liking us now.)

Here is a good time to use our imagination. What else could our audience guess or ask a partner?

Let's think about examples that we can use right away. We can practice them out loud and figure out which ones feel comfortable for us. Or, we can practice them out loud while imagining which example will be the perfect fit for our audience.

#4. Waking up the room.

Sometimes conferences have long sessions with no bathroom breaks. After a few boring speakers, the audience is almost ready for a nap. And then they introduce us.

Think of the audience. Will they judge us cruelly? Of course. They just want their marathon conference to be over. They want to talk to their friends and have a drink. They're tired of sitting. This reminds them of tortuous days sitting for hours in elementary school.

To wake up the room, here is a fun exercise. We will ask everyone in the room to stand up and trade their business cards with ten other people. They can't sit down until they collect ten business cards from their fellow attendees.

However, we need to prime them first. The audience is tired and bored. If we ask everyone to stand up, many will just remain in their seats, stewing in their misery. So how do we prime them?

We will use a little mind-reading trick. Yes, we are going to read their minds. Here is what we will say:

"I know you have been sitting through a long, long session so far. You would love to get up and stretch." (Yes, we have read their minds. That wasn't so hard.)

"So we are going to get that chance in a moment. Here is what we need to do:

"Pull out ten of your business cards. If you don't have ten, than ask yourself, 'How big are my dreams?'

"We are going to exchange our ten business cards with ten other people in the room.

"Now, if you don't have ten personal business cards, at least collect ten cards from others. You will want to carry more business cards with you in the future, especially if you don't want to limit your prospecting opportunities.

"Once you have collected ten new business cards, we will review them. We will look for the secret to why some business cards work, and others go into the trash.

"So, are we ready? Let's stand up, look around, and gather ten business cards from your fellow attendees."

This little mini-speech of instructions gives the audience time to think, "Hey, I do want to get up and stretch. Maybe say a few words to people instead of just sitting here pretending to take notes." Our chances of compliance increase when we give clear instructions. When we tell them the reason why we are doing the exercise, this gives them a few moments to digest the thought of standing up and participating.

#5. "What is your biggest fear? Tell it to a partner!"

We have to know our group and if this is appropriate. Some "stiffer" groups, such as bankers, won't show this side of themselves to another person. But if we have a group of New Age tree-huggers, they might love this exercise. Knowing our audience is important.

Now everyone is judging their partner, not us.

Telling another person something secret or very personal creates a strong bond. Our audience will feel more like a select group of comrades, different than those outsiders who didn't participate in this exercise.

The plus-side of this exercise is that it is interesting. Listen to some of the fears rational people have such as:

* Fear of spiders.

* Fear of flying.

* Fear of bugs.

* Fear of shaking hands.

* Fear of heights.

* Fear of public speaking.

* Fear of sharing one's fears.

* Fear of meeting new people.

* Fear of being judged.

If we think this opening is too aggressive, we can prime the audience by telling them some of our fears, or fears that other groups shared. People will feel more comfortable sharing fears when they know they are not alone.

#6. "Grab a pen. We are only going to write down a few words. That's it. (So we better make these words memorable!) Here is the situation. Your potential customer calls you and says, 'Okay, in one sentence, tell me why I should do business with you.' Now write down your one-sentence answer."

In this exercise, we didn't say, "What is the first sentence you would say when you meet a prospect?" That is too vague. They could imagine a friendly prospect, or a mean prospect. They could think of last week's cold prospect, or even a social contact. If the exercise is vague or confusing, people won't participate. They are afraid of getting it wrong.

That is why we specified that it was the prospect calling, and the prospect asked a specific question. The prospect expects a simple one-sentence answer.

Here is what will happen with this exercise. The audience will see their words in writing. No fumbling, no excuses. No way of saying that "it would depend on the situation."

Once they have written down their sentence, ask them to trade their piece of paper with a partner. Yes, more interaction. And then we could ask them if they wanted to keep their partner's sentence, or get their original sentence back.

Want to try humor? We could say:

"If you passed your partner a blank sheet of paper... your partner is going to look pretty silly saying nothing the next time he or she is asked that question."

And now our presentation can begin on how to have better responses. We established the problem in the audience's minds, and now they are waiting for us to provide a solution.

What if our audience is a challenge? What if we have a cold audience that might resist writing down that response?

Then, we could give examples of bad responses before asking them to write down their best answer. Our examples could be so bad that they would laugh. That takes the pressure off the audience. Now, they won't feel intimidated trying to write down their own answers.

#7. "Filling your bucket list with things to do is exciting. Share with your partner two of the amazing things you want to do."

A bucket list usually contains things "cool" people dream about accomplishing. Limiting beliefs can stop people from building their own lists. Other times, lack of money and time keeps postponing the bucket lists.

Our audience will enjoy sharing their dreams of flying first-class to Europe, climbing Mount Kilimanjaro, skydiving, or visiting the Smithsonian Museum. Talking about dreams makes us more enthusiastic and energetic. Good things for our audience to feel.

Collective exercises for the group to do together.

Not every exercise will fit our style or group. But the more exercises we have in our arsenal, the more choices and variety we will have.

Why use group exercises?

Sometimes we will have a percentage of attendees who want to fold their arms and scowl. Okay, their lives are already miserable. They won't feel like participating in any questions or exercises. But if this is a group exercise, the social pressure from others can help some of these negative people to get involved.

Here are two quick examples.

#1. "I need four volunteers to raise your hand. Okay. You will be the four group leaders. Please stand up so everyone can see you. Now, let's divide ourselves into four groups. Try to make the four groups as even as possible."

Well, even the negative people will have to walk over to be in one of the groups. Participation is happening. And, they are all wondering what is going to happen.

#2. "Starting with the front row, with this person on the left. Please write down one word, and then pass the piece of paper to the next person. The next person will add a word to continue the sentence. Then, continue passing the paper on to the next person. By the time this paper reaches the back of the room, we should have a miniature story written by each side of the room."

Now, if our talk was about the collective intelligence of groups, this will be an interesting exercise for them. And, you might have a fun story by the time each side of the room has finished their writing.

Want more participation? Introduce a little competition. Say, "And at the end of my talk, I will read the stories from each side of the room. Then we will vote on which side of the room had the most interesting story."

Use exercises whenever you can.

This book is only about the first 20 seconds of our presentation. Our goal is getting the prospect to focus, not on us, but on our message.

However, don't limit the exercises in our presentations to only the first 20 seconds. Exercises are a great way to keep the audience continuously involved.

After a coffee break, after lunch, when you are introduced as a speaker after dinner at a conference...

Any time is a great time for an exercise.

So here are another 21 examples of exercises that we can do later in our presentation to raise the energy or to make a point.

21 more exercises to keep our audience interested.

1. "Write down the name of one person in your childhood who said you couldn't succeed. Then share how you felt about them with a partner."

Most everyone will have one critic in their life. We don't forget our critics.

2. "Pass this ball around the room and describe an activity you could do with it."

This exercise takes about 5 to 10 minutes depending on the size of the room. Good for stimulating creative thinking. A nice way to start up again after a break with an audience that is already familiar with you.

3. "Give the person beside you a compliment that has nothing to do with how they look."

You will break the ice as they talk to each other and say something positive. It is a great way to get people smiling and feeling good.

4. "Make a paper plane in the next 60 seconds and prepare to see whose plane will fly the longest distance."

Fun activity, usually worth doing just before a coffee break or lunch. Lightens the mood and uses up to ten minutes. You can line people up. Do it in pairs, have a full competition, or do it in one go!

5. "Take one of the candies in this bag and pass it along."

Reciprocity. Use when you want people to be listening and not talking. Talking is hard to do with their mouths full! But it is also an example of giving before getting. When you make the effort to give your audience a gift, no matter how small it is, they feel obliged to respond positively and give back. And the size of the gift doesn't matter.

6. "Get into a group of three people and, in the next 60 seconds, see if you can create a cool motivational quote."

Then, give a few examples of some quotes. This is a great way to get people out of theory and into practice.

7. "Stand up and write down a rough guess of how many people in this room are older than you, and younger than you."

Our audience is looking around the room frantically trying to guess an accurate number. Yes, our audience has forgotten about judging us.

8. "Turn to the person beside you and ask them where they think they will be in 12 months."

Now goal-setting is getting personal. The audience is thinking. And because they are asking each other, there is no pressure from us on the stage.

9. "Form a group of four people. You will create a story, but you will create your story one word at a time. Each person says a word, and then it is the next person's turn. So after four words, four people will have spoken."

Great creativity exercise and usually quite funny. We can set the topic, and it will help make the point that everyone is thinking of something different. Some of the outcomes are hilarious and insightful. Share the results with the whole group.

10. "Find a partner and ask them, 'What is the best tip you have learned so far?'"

This is great if we are running out of material, but there is plenty of time left. We will now have a bit of time to plan the next segment, or to regain our train of thought. And our audience is talking about what they liked best from what you have taught them so far.

11. "Write down three tips you have learned so far today."

Writing exercises engage the sense of feeling or touch. Our audience can now "do" something instead of just watching us. Need more time? Then ask them to discuss their best tips with their partners. This assures you that everyone is taking home at least three tips from our talk.

12. "Stand up and stretch."

A simple exercise to get the blood flowing. Not recommended in the first 20 seconds with a cold audience that doesn't know you. We might be taking some grumpy people outside of their comfort zone if we ask them to do this right away.

When people stand, they become more alert, which means we have a more engaged audience. Want to have a little fun? Ask them to just stretch one side of their body to see if they can feel the difference.

13. "Please turn to page 17 in your workbook and complete the two questions."

Make sure the two questions are short and easy. And, be ready to introduce an interesting sentence to get them to reconnect with you.

14. "Please take one worksheet and hand the rest across the room so everybody has one."

This is a simple but effective way of breaking the ice in the room, especially if they don't know each other. People will be polite, passing the pile of worksheets, and those receiving them will say thank you.

15. "Pull out your phone and take a photo of yourself here at the conference. Next, upload it to this Facebook page. Later, we will vote on the craziest photo."

If you have a fun-loving audience, they are going to love you.

16. "Pull out your phone and post a comment about having fun here at the conference."

This is what is often described as "riding the horse in the direction the horse is going." People will never put their phones away in this day and age. So encourage them to use them. Taking photos, posting updates, tweeting... it is all about creating buzz for your message or event.

17. "Go to the App Store and download the free XYZ app. It will take only 30 seconds. Then, we are going to do something awesome."

Instructing people to get a free app is a form of exercise that combines the technology and learning. They already have the phone in their hands. Now they are wondering what the awesome application will be.

18. "Grab a pen and paper or your phone, and list three people on your team who should have been here today."

This is a simple exercise that spreads the word to more people about your message. If you have a worksheet or a sales sheet you can even encourage them to get it off your website and share it with those missing people immediately!

19. "Please raise your hand if you like Chinese food."

This is a simple exercise that allows us to get people moving. The act of raising the hand goes back to kindergarten. It is polite and it is subtle. This takes the audience back to their past when they took instructions and listened to the teacher.

20. "Write a compliment down on a piece of paper and give it to the person beside you."

Giving a gift makes people feel good. This is usually less confronting than verbally giving a compliment. However, the delayed reaction is priceless.

21. "Turn to your partner and take note of the color of your partner's eyes."

Then we can survey the room for the percentage of people who have blue eyes, brown eyes, etc. Maybe our personal research discovered certain traits people have for each color.

Exercises work.

As we can see, exercises can come in many different forms. The bottom line: get the audience involved and engaged.

Exercises help the audience bond. That is a good thing, especially if our audience is a group of strangers. And exercises can help the audience focus on our message.

Let's review.

Now we have three great shortcuts to help us open our speech and get the audience engaged.

#1. Ask a question.

#2. Tell a story.

#3. Use an exercise.

If we use one of these three shortcuts, our audience will lean forward and focus on our message.

What about us? Much of our fear and nervousness will disappear as our audience concentrates on our message instead of us.

What about after the first 20 seconds?

Well, it gets easier. Now we have the audience on our side.

Of course there are many more skills needed to become a professional and polished public speaker. However, getting the first 20 seconds right gives us the best chance of success.

So let's practice these three great shortcuts. And the next time we give a speech, we can feel prepared and confident from the moment we open our mouths.

YOU MIGHT ALSO ENJOY THESE BOOKS:

Start SuperNetworking! 5 Simple Steps to Creating Your Own Personal Networking Group

by Keith Schreiter and Tom "Big Al" Schreiter

The best salesmen and the best business owners have strong personal networks.

Whether you are a small business, a network marketer, or a professional salesman, prospects that have been pre-sold by your personal networking group make your business easy and enjoyable.

Once you have this business model in place, you will never go back to the old ways of prospecting, advertising and marketing your business again.

How To Get Instant Trust, Belief, Influence and Rapport! 13 Ways To Create Open Minds By Talking To The Subconscious Mind

by Tom "Big Al" Schreiter

Use these tested, clear techniques to build that instant rapport with other people and then, everything else is easy.

If you are a leader, a salesman, a network marketer, an influencer, a teacher, or someone who needs to communicate quickly and efficiently, this book is for you.

Both books available at:

http://BigAlBooks.com

ABOUT MARK DAVIS

Mark Davis is an international speaker and trainer whose passion is to inspire people to grow, lead and connect.

His courses on public speaking have helped thousands of people across the world become more confident and more effective communicators.

Mark is also passionate about coaching, travelling and making a positive social impact.

Contact Mark at:

Mark@MasterTheArtOfPublicSpeaking.com

ABOUT TOM SCHREITER

Tom "Big Al" Schreiter has 40+ years of experience in network marketing and MLM. He conducts workshops worldwide, and has authored numerous books.

His passion is marketing ideas, marketing campaigns, and how to speak to the subconscious mind in simplified, practical ways.

Tom is a favorite speaker at company conventions and regional events.

Contact Tom at:

BigAlNews@FortuneNow.com

46929624R00061

Made in the USA
Lexington, KY
01 August 2019